To: You, From: Me

A collection of words never sent.

Riley Capritto

BookLeaf Publishing

India | USA | UK

Dedication

To you,
The one who gave me a love of dizzying highs and
devastating lows,
a connection so deep it still lingers in the quiet corners
of my heart.
These poems are for the love we shared,
the moments that lifted me, and the ones that shattered
me.
But they are also for the love I tried to find after you,
hoping to feel whole again,
and the love I'm still searching for,
somewhere between the fragments of who I was and
who I'm becoming.
This book is my truth, written for anyone who knows
the beauty and ache of giving their heart away.

Preface

Love is rarely simple. It lifts us to heights we never imagined and leaves us aching in ways we never thought possible. This book is a testament to both—the dizzying highs of a deep connection and the heartbreak that comes when it slips away.

Some of these poems are for the love that first taught me to dream and then to break, the one who remains etched into my heart despite the passage of time. Others are for the love I sought afterward, the people who taught me to try again, to hope again, even when my heart was still finding its pieces.

And then, there are the poems for the love I am still searching for, the one I know is out there, waiting to remind me why we risk so much for something so fragile.

This collection is my way of making sense of it all—the joy, the pain, the longing, and the lessons. I hope as you read these words, you see yourself in them, too. Because love, in all its forms, is what connects us, even when it breaks us apart.

Acknowledgements

This book would not exist without the love and support of the people who have walked alongside me through life's highest highs and lowest lows.

To my mom and dad: Thank you for teaching me the value of resilience. Your unwavering belief in me has been the foundation of everything I do.

To my best friend, Amber: You've been my anchor and my light. Thank you for being there through every moment—big and small—and for always reminding me of my worth, even when I couldn't see it myself.

To Sofia B., Julie H., Daphne S., and Sophia S.: Your kindness, encouragement, support and friendship have meant more than words can express.

And to you, the reader: Thank you for holding these words in your hands and allowing me to share my story with you. I hope these pages offer you comfort, understanding, or simply the reminder that you're not alone.

With all my love and gratitude,
Riley

Beginning of the End

The clock whispered secrets we refused to hear,
A quiet unraveling, year by year.
What once was golden began to rust,
Love buried beneath the weight of dust.
In that final year, the cracks grew wide,
Fueled by storms you could no longer hide.
The drunken words, sharp and unkind,
Left bruises on more than my fragile mind.
Promises tumbled from your lips with ease,
Empty as the bottles that brought me to my knees.
"I'll change," you'd swear, your voice a vow,
But nothing ever changed—not then, not now.
Your outbursts echoed through the hollow night,
Leaving love shattered in the morning light.
I clung to hope like a fraying rope,
But the knots unraveled with every "nope."
We tried to mend, to heal the pain,
But your anger poured like relentless rain.
Each drunken rage a nail in the coffin,
Each apology forgotten, too often.
I gave you my patience, my tears, my all,
But I couldn't save us from the fall.
Your words were weapons, your promises chains,
And I was left holding the weight of your pain.

So the last year wrote our goodbye,
A tale of sorrow, too broken to try.
Not with anger, not with hate,
But with the knowledge we couldn't escape our fate.
Now I walk away with scars that fade,
And lessons learned in the mess we made.
The beginning of the end was harsh but true:
Loving myself meant letting go of you.

The Weight of His Wounds

We built a world of whispered dreams,
Laughter echoing through fragile seams.
In your arms, I found a fleeting peace,
Yet in your shadow, I felt release.
The love between us, fierce and deep,
A tide so strong, it lulled to sleep
The voices warning, quiet, low—
The signs of storms I'd come to know.
You carried wounds you couldn't name,
Ghosts of the past you tried to tame.
But in their haunt, they lashed at me,
A captive soul, I longed to be free.
Each word, a blade, though softly thrown,
Cut deep, yet left me all alone.
I held you close, my trembling hands,
Begging you to break your chains.
I saw the light within your eyes,
A spark that fought the bitter lies.
But you turned away, refused to heal,
Chose your pain over what was real.
I bore the weight, I bore it long,
Hoped that love could right the wrong.
But love, it seems, can't mend a heart
That won't let healing even start.

So here I stand, the tide now gone,
A battered soul, but not alone.
I loved you fiercely, gave my all,
But no one wins when shadows fall.
And though our love was deep, profound,
It couldn't lift what held you bound.
I walk away, my heart still sore,
But I won't carry your wounds anymore.

The Moment We Met

The moment we met, the air shifted,
As though time paused, and the world tilted.
Your eyes held stories my soul seemed to know,
A spark ignited, a connection aglow.
From the start, the road was uneven,
A love that burned hot, fierce, and uneven.
But oh, how I loved you, deeply, desperately,
Clinging to hope when the storms met me.
For eight and a half years, we fought and we mended,
A tangled bond, both broken and blended.
Through laughter and tears, I gave you my all,
Even as cracks threatened our wall.
I felt it then, deep in my core,
You'd be a chapter, perhaps even more.
A tether unseen, drawing me near,
Familiarity wrapped in wonder and fear.
But life is a river, forever in flow,
And not all connections are destined to grow.
You came like the sunrise, warm and bright,
Then faded away into the night.
Not meant to stay, though I begged fate,
Our love was a lesson wrapped in ache.
Eight and a half—a love so true,
A chapter closed, but I'll always hold you.

The Fire I Could Never Put Out

I ran through storms with bare, blistered feet,
Left warmth and laughter for the cold of his cry,
Chased his chaos, a heart in retreat,
While my own needs were left to die.
I watched my reflection blur and fade,
In puddles of tears I could never show,
Every sacrifice a card I played,
To prove the love he should already know.
Nights became battlegrounds soaked in flame,
A carousel spinning, dizzy with dread,
I whispered devotion, called out his name,
As the fire raged inside my head.
I told him of my love—again, again,
Pleading with a voice that cracked and bled,
Surely this time he'd see through his pain,
That the bond I offered was not misread.
Hours stretched thin, agony's choke,
Until the flames began to die,
His anger dimmed at the words I spoke,
As if love could be a lullaby.
The fire was out—at last, at cost,
Smoke curled like shadows against the dawn,
But deep in my gut, I knew I'd lost,

For this was a ride I couldn't stay on.
Round and round, the sickness grew,
His peace was fleeting, my pain stayed,
And though I had pleaded my love as true,
I was the one who always paid.

Fleeting Magic

I remember the magic, like gold-dusted air,
Moments with you, when nothing compared.
The laughter, the closeness, the warmth of your smile,
Felt like eternity, though it lasted a while.
Your touch turned the mundane to starlit nights,
Every word you spoke ignited soft lights.
We danced in a world spun from whispers and dreams,
A fragile enchantment, or so it now seems.
But shadows would creep, silent and sly,
Planting false whispers that darkened the sky.
You'd weave a new story, of wrongs never done,
A tempest within, eclipsing our sun.
And then you would push, retreat into stone,
Trying to leave me, to be on your own.
But I, in my yearning, would beg you to stay,
To hold on to love, not let it decay.
Over and over, this cycle took hold,
For 8.5 years, through warm and through cold.
The magic would flicker, then sputter, then die,
Revived by my pleading, yet fragile as sighs.
Still, I can't forget how alive I once felt,
In the glow of the world where together we dwelt.
Those moments were fleeting, like fireflies' gleam,
A beautiful nightmare, a broken dream.

Now I hold the magic, and also the pain,
The weight of the joy and the ache of the rain.
I know that it's over, but still, in my mind,
I'll cherish the moments when love felt kind.

Only Me and You

In the hush of the night, where the world withdrew,
There was nothing—only me and you.
A collision of need, raw and untamed,
Two bodies aflame, no words could name.
Every touch was a spark, electric, wild,
A storm unleashed, reckless and riled.
Your breath on my skin, a sacred prayer,
A promise of passion beyond compare.
We climbed to heights I didn't know,
Through peaks of pleasure, we let it flow.
The universe folded, the stars burned bright,
As we lost ourselves in endless night.
Now I wonder, with a heart so torn,
If that heat, that bond, can ever be reborn.
Was that moment ours, a fleeting dream,
A love so fierce it split the seams?
For in your arms, the world felt right,
A fire eternal in the depth of the night.
And though the future may yet unfold,
That flame, with you, is forever gold.

Fool's Love

The memory lingers, sharp and raw,
A quiet betrayal, the truth I foresaw.
Her words weren't much, just a fleeting line,
But they echoed a story that wasn't mine.
"Missing you," she wrote, bold and clear,
And suddenly, the sickness you claimed felt insincere.
Yet still, I clung to the hope, paper-thin,
That this wasn't a battle I couldn't win.
Then came the screenshot—her face, your grin,
The screen between you too fragile, too thin.
A late-night call I wasn't meant to see,
Proof of the distance that grew between you and me.
Did anything happen? I'll never quite know,
But suspicion has roots, and they always grow.
The fear you'd strayed, yet again, to her side,
Was a weight in my chest I couldn't divide.
Still, I stayed, a fool for your name,
Burning in silence, engulfed in the flame.
I told myself love was a battle to prove,
A maze with no end, a heart I couldn't move.
I gave you devotion, unwavering and blind,
A love that consumed both my heart and my mind.
Even as doubt took root in my soul,
I bent myself backwards to make you feel whole.

What madness it was to fight for the pain,
To weather your storms, to stand in the rain.
But love made me foolish, made me believe,
That your fleeting attention was something to achieve.
And though I knew deep down, clear as the sea,
That you weren't the man you pretended to be,
I stayed in the shadow of your reckless youth,
Chasing a love that denied me the truth.

A Prisoner Of His Control

I held my breath to quiet the storm,
While his rage took on its cruelest form.
Words like knives, they cut so deep,
Echoes of anger that stole my sleep.
The weight of his words sank into my skin,
Each threat to leave, a war within.
I shrank, consumed by the ache inside,
Pleading for love while my body died.
He cursed my name, called me less than whole,
Yet I begged, a prisoner of his control.
"I'm sorry," I whispered for sins untrue,
For crimes he conjured, for lies he drew.
Each time he swore to walk away,
My heart collapsed; I'd plead, I'd stay.
The mirror revealed what I couldn't deny—
A fragile shell, fading by and by.
Panic took me where hunger dared not,
An anxious fire that burned and fought.
Every meal became a distant ghost,
Every pound lost, his unholy boast.
But still, I clung, though I was breaking,
A fool for love, my soul forsaking.
To make him see he was my sun,
Though in his shadow, I came undone.

Now I stand, a survivor of war,
Reclaiming the body he made so sore.
The weight of his anger, I've cast away,
And found the strength to greet each day.
For though I bent, I did not break,
From his ashes, my own wings I make.
And if love means losing all you are,
Then I've found something brighter by far.

The Chains You Wore So Easily

You clung to me like rust on iron,
Corroding every moment I sought to be free.
A night with friends turned into a trial,
Your accusations hung heavy—chains only I could see.
My laughter would barely echo
Before your voice filled the void,
Spewing doubts you conjured,
My joy reduced to something you'd destroy.
Each ring of the phone was a siren's wail,
Your words, sharp as glass, tore through my night.
A hostage to your paranoia,
Every step away from you felt like a fight.
But when the roles reversed,
And it was your turn to roam,
You slipped through shadows, unanswered,
While I waited, staring at the screen alone.
You rewrote your whereabouts,
Twisting truth to fit your needs.
I swallowed every lie,
While my heart bled from unseen deeds.
I begged for fairness, for balance, for peace,
But you thrived in the chaos you'd sewn.
I was leashed by your insecurities,

While you danced freely, as if none were your own.
Now I see those chains for what they were—
A reflection of your own despair.
You sought control, not love,
And left me gasping for air.
So here's to the nights I'll reclaim,
To laughter untainted by your demands.
I've broken free of your weight,
And I'll never let you touch my light again.

Turning Joy Into Sin

It was just a laugh,
a harmless sound,
a joke from a friend
that wasn't even clever.
But his eyes darkened,
his jaw set like a trap,
and I knew the storm was here.
"Stop acting like a hoe," he snapped,
each word a dagger,
cold steel sinking into my chest.
"Show me some respect," he growled,
as if I had stolen something
sacred from him
with a smile meant for someone else.
It wasn't about the joke.
It never was.
It was about control,
about his need to shrink me
down to fit inside
his fragile pride.
His love—if that's what it was—
was a leash,
tightening every time
I dared to exist outside his reach.

I stopped laughing then,
swallowed the sound
like bitter medicine.
And still, he said he loved me,
in the quiet hours
when the rage subsided,
when his hands sought mine
as if forgiveness
was as simple as holding on.
But love, when real,
doesn't silence laughter
or turn joy into sin.
It doesn't weaponize respect
or tear down trust
to build its throne.
Yet I stayed silent,
waiting for the storm to pass,
knowing it would come again.

A Night Of Screaming

It began with a shadow,
just a name, a faint trace,
a relic of a time long buried,
a boy who never held his place.
But your anger rose like a tidal wave,
fueled by ghosts I never called.
Each word became a crashing blow,
and I stood, breaking, small.
In the parking lot, under flickering lights,
I held my breath, my hands, your pain.
But every plea I whispered softly
only fed the growing flame.
Your rage was a storm, relentless, wild,
it turned the night into a fight.
And I, drowning, tried to reach you,
but you sank deeper out of sight.
On the freeway, the lines dissolved,
the night became a reckless blur.
Our voices clashed like shattered glass,
your rage my fear, a tragic stir.
We drove too fast, too far, too raw,
fueled by anger, liquor, despair.
The stars above were silent witnesses
to a bond unraveling in the air.

And when the silence finally came,
it wasn't peace—it was the cost.
The ash of love, the wreck of trust,
a night of screaming, all we'd lost.

I Knew When I Asked

You stood before me, eyes steady and clear,
Swearing truths I was desperate to hear.
A question hung heavy, my heart in its place,
"Have you been watching?"
I saw the twitch, the flicker of doubt,
The way your gaze darted, seeking a way out.
Your words fell too perfect, rehearsed to a tee,
But I heard the cracks in your frail alibi.
A chance, a gift, to come clean, to be true,
To say, "Yes, it's me; I've been watching you."
But no—your lie came, smooth and precise,
Your tongue choosing shadows over the light.
And then, when the strings of us had snapped,
When the story of us had been gently wrapped,
You came crawling, not as yourself,
But cloaked in deceit from your hidden shelf.
A message sent from a ghost I'd met,
Spilling truths you hoped I'd forget.
"It was me," you confessed, "all along,
The watcher, the liar, the one in the wrong."
And more—your plea, so desperate, so bare,
"Don't move on yet. Don't let someone else care."
You begged from the shadows for one last delay,
As if my healing could wait, could obey.

How small you must feel in your house of lies,
Building walls of deceit, while your conscience cries.
For what is love if not raw, exposed?
Not hidden, not masked, not poorly composed.
I knew when I asked, the truth in my gut,
That you'd weave a story, try to keep the door shut.
But the truth has a way of breaking through,
And now all you are is a lesson I knew.
Lies may shield, but they can't repair,
The trust once built with tender care.
So beg from the shadows, it won't change a thing—
I've closed the door. Let the truth finally sting.

A Fleeting Enchantment

It started with laughter, a casual night,
A group of friends bathed in dim, buzzing light.
The air grew electric with stories and cheers,
Fueled by the warmth of spirits and beers.
But somewhere between the jokes and the sway,
I noticed your glance, then I looked away.
A tether unseen, a pull in the air,
An unspoken question hung, bold yet rare.
The night spiraled onward, chaotic and bright,
Yet your presence grew vivid, eclipsing the night.
We drifted together, as if by design,
Two strangers with fates that briefly aligned.
We talked about her—your love, your care,
But a spark whispered secrets I didn't dare share.
Your words felt like puzzles, each piece held a glow,
Hints of a longing you might never show.
Closer we leaned, as if gravity knew,
That something was brewing, forbidden but true.
And when it was over, we parted, yet stayed,
In that moment of magic our silence conveyed.
I turned back to glimpse, unsure what I'd see,
But there you were, also looking at me.
Our eyes locked, and time seemed to pause,
A smile, a blush, a moment without cause.

The night left a mark, a question, a flame,
A fleeting enchantment with no one to blame.
I wonder if you felt the same pull too,
Or if magic, that night, was mine to pursue.
So I carry it gently, this spark in my chest,
A memory treasured, a night so blessed.
Though life moves ahead, that glow will remain,
A bittersweet wonder I'll never explain.

A Spark Revisited

A year had passed, yet there he stood,
like a memory made flesh, a whisper of good.
The air between us hummed, electric and bright,
as if time had only deepened the light.
Big smiles broke across our faces wide,
like reflections in a mirror, no need to hide.
Laughter spilled out, soft and free,
filling the space where tension should be.
And then—a high five, so simple, so small,
but it lingered, like a question, like a call.
Fingers brushed, a spark ignited anew,
a fleeting connection, too good to be true.
I wonder, in the quiet of my mind,
if he too feels the pull, the bind.
Does he think of that moment, of what could be?
Or am I the keeper of this memory?
Years have gone, yet sometimes I see
his smile in dreams, what we might be.
A love that never had its chance to start,
still holding a corner of my heart.

The Day You Took What Was Mine

It was supposed to be a day
drenched in joy,
a celebration of my triumph,
of the doors I pried open with sweat,
with tears,
with dreams no one but me
truly understood.
I got into grad school—
my grad school.
The one I whispered to the stars about,
the one I fought to believe I deserved.
The plans were set:
a dinner, lights, laughter,
toasting the next chapter of my life.
But then—
you found my journal,
my sacred space.
Words I'd written for myself,
not for you,
became the target of your fury.
You read them,
twisted them,
threw them back at me

like they were weapons meant to wound.
The anger you unleashed
wasn't about my words,
it wasn't about me.
It was the weight of your own shadows
seeking a place to land.
I stood there,
the joy of the day wilting,
shrinking under the heat of your rage.
What should have been a night
for celebration
became a void of broken plans—
calls canceled, candles unlit,
and my heart, heavy with disbelief.
That was when I knew.
I looked at you and saw
not the partner I deserved
but the storm I had weathered for too long.
This day,
my day,
would not be defined by your anger.
So I said the words
I'd been afraid to say:
"It's over."
And though the silence afterward
was loud and raw,
I found peace in it.

Because the celebration was never yours to ruin—
it was mine to reclaim.

28

The Final Embrace

We stood, tangled in the final embrace,
hearts breaking in a quiet place.
Our tears spoke words we couldn't say,
as time pushed him further away.
The rain began, soft and cold,
a symphony of stories untold.
I watched the car fade into gray,
until the world took him away.
Drops fell heavy, matched my cries,
clouds wept too, from aching skies.
It felt as though the earth could see,
the hollowed-out remains of me.
I wandered through the hours, lost,
counting love and weighing the cost.
Though I knew the end was right,
my soul still broke in endless night.
He lingers still, in every thought,
the lessons learned, the battles fought.
Yet, parts of me refuse to heal,
the ache too sharp, too deeply real.
Perhaps this pain will ebb and wane,
perhaps the sun will pierce the rain.
But for now, I carry the sting,
and the memory of everything.

The Breaking Point

The doctor called with numbers
that didn't add up,
words like "unusual"
sharp enough to make me tremble.
Blood betrayed what I wouldn't say,
whispering secrets of a body
breaking under weight it couldn't carry.
Scans followed,
cold machines tracing the truth:
my liver, weary and worn,
faltered under the burden
of everything you left behind.
The years of abuse etched into my mind
had found a home beneath my skin.
"Complex PTSD," they said.
But how do you explain
a trauma so heavy
it scars the organs that keep you alive?
How do you heal
when the damage is written
in the language of cells and enzymes?
California held my last gasp of normalcy—
a string of moments with friends,
a frantic attempt to salvage joy

before I left for the unknown.
I smiled as my body starved,
forced laughter past the nausea,
held tight to fleeting embraces
like they could anchor me.
But the mirror told the truth:
a shadow of myself stared back,
skin stretched too thin
over a skeleton that couldn't hold me.
I hated her.
I hated what you'd done.
I hated the years of pain
that refused to let me go.
The cross-country move was survival,
an escape from ghosts
that had taken root in familiar streets.
But even distance couldn't sever
the ties between my mind and my body.
Complex PTSD—
not just in thoughts,
but in flesh and blood,
in the quiet suffering of a liver
that bore my pain
when I could no longer bear it alone.
Pills became my lifeline,
medicine for a soul too raw to heal
on its own.

And yet, beneath it all,
a flicker of resilience—
a body that refused to give up,
a heart that kept beating
despite the scars it carried.
You broke me, yes,
but I am not just what you left behind.
I am the nights I survived,
the mornings I fought to rise,
the strength it took to leave
and start again.
The scans told a story of damage,
but they also told a story of life,
of a body fighting to keep me here,
of a will that wouldn't be extinguished.
I am still here.
And I am learning to forgive
the girl who stayed too long,
the girl who fought to leave,
the girl who now refuses to give up.

A Witness To Love

I watched the rings find their rightful place,
Each promise etched in a joyful face.
Amber's hand held Sean's with care,
Their engagement a bond beyond compare.
Then came Tim, my cousin, my kin,
Elisa by his side, a love deep within.
Their announcement came with laughter and cheer,
A moment so bright, so perfectly clear.
Not long after, Daphne and Tyler shared,
Their engagement glowing, their love declared.
Each photo, each story, each gleaming ring,
A chorus of joy, a song they could sing.
I was happy for them, how could I not be?
Their love stories bloomed like blossoms on trees.
I clapped and I cheered, my heart truly glad,
For the love they had found, the dreams they now had.
Yet in their glow, I stayed apart,
Convinced that love wasn't meant for my heart.
Not bitter, not angry, just quietly sure,
That my story of love had closed its door.
For them, engagement was a spark, a new start,
For me, it felt like a foreign art.
Amber and Sean, so perfectly matched,
Daphne and Tyler, their futures attached.

I stood in the wings, a silent observer,
A witness to love, but not its deserter.
Their joy was real, their bonds were true,
But love, I believed, was not my due.
Still, I smiled, my applause sincere,
For their futures so bright, their paths so clear.
Even if rings never circle my hand,
I'll cherish their stories and still understand.

The Spaces Between

I used to know who I was,
barefoot in California sun,
hair loose, arms wide,
a girl shaped by salt air and wanderlust.
The ocean cradled my dreams,
its tide a steady rhythm
to match my own.
But then I left,
heart bruised and heavy,
and the freeway faded into flatlands,
into skies that stretched too quiet.
Ohio greeted me with cold hands,
its winters sharp,
its summers unfamiliar.
The girl I was couldn't find her footing
on this foreign ground.
For a while,
I mourned her—
her laughter, her ease,
the way she belonged to the world
and herself.
I wore her like a memory
too tight for my skin,
trying to fit back into a version of me

that didn't live here anymore.
But time doesn't wait.
It layers itself like seasons,
each one softer than the last.
And in those seasons,
I grew roots.
Not like the palms of California,
but like oaks—
sturdy, slow, reaching deep.
Now I see her in glimpses:
the boho girl,
still dreaming,
still free.
But she's joined by someone new—
someone who knows the quiet power
of showing up,
of pushing through the frost
to bloom again.
I am her,
both of them,
all of them.
A mix of sun and snow,
of the wild child and the grounded woman.
And here, in this middle place,
I am learning to love
the spaces between.

I Thought You Were Different

I hate how you shifted, how quickly you changed,
How your interest in me just faded, estranged.
From warm conversations and laughter so sweet,
To silence that echoes, a ghost on repeat.
I hate how you made me feel seen, understood,
How I thought you were different, I thought you were good.
You painted a future, then left it undone,
Now I'm haunted by memories of what we'd begun.
I hate how you vanished, how sudden, how cold,
How I'm stuck wondering at stories untold.
How could someone who seemed to care so completely
Leave me questioning worth, feeling small and defeated?
I hate that I search for the reasons you left,
How I comb through each moment, confused and bereft.
Was it something I said, or did I fall too fast?
How did interest like ours fade away into past?
I hate that I miss the connection we shared,
That I cared far too much while you hardly seemed scared.
From feeling so special, so noticed, so real,
To nothing at all, just a void I still feel.

Seeds That Never Grew

You pulled the world from under my feet,
Whispered dreams that tasted sweet,
Spun promises with careful hands,
Built a future on shifting sands.
I fell hard, without a net,
Trusting you without regret,
You painted love like constellations,
A universe of our creation.
But now those stars have lost their glow,
The light replaced by what I know:
Your words were seeds that never grew,
Empty soil, a barren view.
How dare you weave a dream so deep,
Where heart and hope both dared to leap?
Now I'm haunted by what could be,
Ghosts of love that won't set me free.
I hate you for the weight I bear,
For the days I spent lost in your stare,
For making me love a life unknown,
Then leaving me to face it alone.
Still, beneath the hate, there lies
A hurt that never quite complies,
A wound that whispers, soft and low,
Why did I love what wouldn't grow?

A Pirate's Life

Fine, let the sea become my home,
where love can't find me, tides will roam.
I'll trade my heart for sails and storms,
for winds that keep my spirit warm.
I'll hoist the flag of reckless dreams,
cut ties with love's deceptive schemes.
No more soft words or whispered lies—
just open waves and endless skies.
A pirate's life, a heart unbound,
no promises to drag me down.
I'll find my gold in moonlit foam,
with freedom as my only throne.
Let tempests howl, let sirens sing,
I'll steer my ship, a roguish king.
I'll guard my heart with iron chains,
and let love sink in past remains.
So here I go, wild, drifting free,
a captain of my destiny.
I'll never love nor weep again,
just sail away from where I've been.

How Gullible

How foolish, how naive, how blind,
to think I meant more than passing time.
You dressed your care in sweet disguise,
but truth was hidden in your eyes.
You spun me dreams with practiced ease,
like whispered lies on summer breeze,
and I believed each crafted line,
each empty word you made divine.
How gullible, to trust the spark,
to give you light while feeling dark.
I poured out love, you watched it spill,
and never meant to catch or fill.
You walked away without a sound,
left me to learn what I had found:
a heart misled, a hopeful mess,
caught in the lie of your caress.
How quick you went, how light you tread,
while I was tangled, lost, misled.
Now here I stand, with broken pride,
knowing you never cared inside.

Just Another Distraction

How silly of me to believe in his eyes,
To think there was truth behind all of his lies.
I painted him gentle, I painted him kind,
Ignoring the warning signs etched in my mind.
How foolish I was to hold onto his touch,
To think he could feel, to think he meant much.
I gave him my laughter, my heart, and my trust,
While he let it all crumble, turn fragile to dust.
How naïve of me to mistake empty words,
To weave them in dreams like the songs of the birds.
I thought he saw beauty in who I could be,
But I was a moment, not something to keep.
How childish to hope that he felt something deep,
To wish he'd remember or struggle to sleep.
I see it now clear, I was never the one,
Just another distraction, a phase he could shun.
How silly of me to have given my all,
To believe he would catch me if ever I'd fall.
But love has a way of distorting the truth,
Leaving lessons in loss and the ache of our youth.

You Said You Only Wanted The Best For Me

Remember when you told me
I had nothing to fear,
that every worry, every restless thought
could rest in the comfort of your words?
You only wanted the best for me,
you said, with a sincerity
that felt like shelter.
I held on to those promises,
let them wrap around my heart,
trusted that your care
was a constant, unbreakable thread.
You were the safety I leaned into,
a hand reaching out when shadows grew.
But now, your silence stretches wide,
a cold absence where warmth once lived.
You walk past me, eyes unseeing,
as if I am nothing more than a stranger,
forgotten, erased from the world you built.
I wonder if you know the weight
of a vanished promise,
how the echoes of your kindness
now haunt more than comfort,
how the fear you told me to bury

has come back with a sharper edge.
You only wanted the best for me,
but now you leave me here,
untethered, sifting through memories,
trying to understand how care
could ever dissolve so completely.

His Voice Turned Gray

He called me every night, without fail,
Soft whispers winding through the dark,
We'd paint dreams on the ceiling, carve our tales,
And promise that no distance could leave a mark.
We spoke of everything—fears and hope's spark,
The future unfurled in a million ways,
Where love would guide us, a map in the stars,
And laughter would linger through endless days.
But one day he called, his voice turned gray,
Words heavy as shadows, fractured and dim.
He said that the future had shifted its way,
And I was no longer the light for him.
Now the night feels empty, the silence deep,
Where echoes of promises haunt my sleep.

The Irony

He said he was tired of chasing,
Of footsteps echoing dreams erased,
Where love was a distance he strained to cross,
And effort lost its lingering grace.
I heard the sorrow in his tales,
Of one who gave too little, too late,
So I promised myself to be the flame,
To never let that passion abate.
But how funny it is, how twisted the game,
When I offered more than he knew how to hold,
My love was a current, a river untamed,
And he drowned in a flood I couldn't control.
For he fled from abundance as swiftly as air,
From a fire too fierce, from care that burned,
Where he longed for pursuit but feared being caught,
How strange the way that lessons turn.
Now I ponder the irony woven so deep,
The paradox left in the ashes to bloom,
Where effort was chased yet feared when returned,
And love left marooned in an echoing room.

Unread

I leave your message unopened, whole,
A tether to what used to be,
A ghost of you I still control,
A lie I live, intentionally.
Unread, your words can't cut or fade,
They sit in limbo, almost real,
Suspended where no hurt is made,
Where hope and heartache barely heal.
I keep you there, a silent thread,
A proof that you still reach for me,
Unread, so I am comforted,
Still tied to your uncertainty.
I fear the truth that comes with loss,
The emptiness that follows through,
So I let this illusion gloss
The broken distance left by you.
Unread, you linger, almost mine,
A bittersweet, deceiving art,
Where love stays paused between the lines,
Unread—but never from my heart.

You Set The Pace

You held the wheel with steady hands,
The road beneath us, shifting sands.
Your foot pressed down, the engine roared,
We chased horizons, never bored.
Your voice was sure, your eyes alight,
You set the pace, both day and night.
Each mile a promise, each turn a plan,
Led by you, a confident man.
But then the speed became too much,
You faltered at the slightest touch.
A tremor in the voice I knew,
The brakes slammed down, a sharp, cold cue.
"Too fast," you said, your gaze askew,
As if the pace was set by two.
I sat in silence, heart confused,
Unsure of how to feel, bemused.
Was it not you who steered the ride,
The one who pulled me close, with pride?
Now here we are, abrupt and still,
Paused halfway up an endless hill.
The wheel, once gripped with such control,
Now slipped through fingers, lost its role.
And I, a passenger by chance,
Was left in this uncertain dance.

You built the road, you drew the map,
And now you say it's all a trap?
A journey planned, then called too fast,
By the very hands that held it last.
So here I sit, with questions rife,
About the road, about this life.
And wonder if we'll find a way,
To move again, or if we'll stay.

To Nothing At All

I hate that I miss him, it's a bitter refrain,
A shadowed echo in a storm of pain.
We went from dawn talks and endless nights,
To silence now that blurs the lights.
Once, our words were a bridge, so strong,
Built of laughter, stories, a place we belonged.
But time, like a thief, pulled us apart,
Leaving fragments of a splintered heart.
The hours that stretched with his voice in my ear,
Have emptied to voids where I fear.
The warmth of his presence, the comfort it gave,
Is now just a ghost I can't save.
I hate that I miss him, it's cruel and true,
To hold on to someone who's gone, who withdrew.
From everything we were to this hollow fall,
From talking each day—to nothing at all.

A Familiar Pain

I trace old paths beneath the trees,
Hoping to find the parts of me.
But leaves have fallen, seasons change,
And I am different, rearranged.
Once I was whole, untouched, unscarred,
Before his shadow, before my guard.
Now I rise, a quieter flame,
A familiar pain, but not quite the same.

Pushed Him Away

51

I laughed at myself so he'd laugh too,
Thinking humor might cover what's hollow and true.
But a part of me feared he'd see right through,
The part that doubted I could be loved by you.
And maybe he tired of the endless refrain,
The jokes that hid shadows, the humor and pain.
Now he's gone, and here I stay,
Knowing it was me who pushed him away.

A Rebirth Rising From The Ache

I lost myself in the weight of "we,"
a tangled love, a stormy sea.
Now I walk these shores alone,
seeking pieces I've outgrown.
In the echoes of what used to be,
I'm sifting through what's left of me,
scraping old scars, tracing lines,
learning which pieces are truly mine.
I gave so much, forgot to keep
the parts of me buried deep.
Now I'm digging, unearthing gold,
finding truths that I can hold.
There's beauty in this fractured state,
a rebirth rising from the ache.
I gather fragments, rearrange,
letting go, embracing change.
Slowly, softly, I become whole,
a tapestry, a mended soul.
I am here, and I am free—
finally finding all of me.

Planting Seeds Of Self-Love

I stand in a mirror, my own quiet sea,
A reflection that whispers, "You're learning to be."
Not perfect, not finished, but soft at the seams,
A mosaic of courage and half-woven dreams.
The world taught me patience, though never for me,
I stitched up my heart with threads I could see.
But there are gaps in the weaving, where doubt makes
its home,
And shadows remind me I'm not yet my own.
Still, I rise in the morning, a fighter at heart,
Building a life that is fragile but art.
Each step is uneven, each breath a new song,
Each stumble a lesson that carries me on.
I dream of a hand that will one day appear,
Not to fix all my fractures, but quiet the fear.
A voice that will echo, as gentle as rain,
"Your scars are not broken—they're beauty through
pain."
They won't complete me; that's a task just for me,
But perhaps they'll remind me of all I could be.
And together we'll grow, like vines reaching light,
Entwined in the promise of love and of might.
Until then, I'll nurture this garden within,
Planting seeds of self-love where doubt once had been.

For while I am learning to love who I see,
I hold hope in my heart for love shared, wild, and free.

54

Lessons In Love

She said it so simply,
as if truth dripped from her lips
like honey meant to sweeten my wounds:
"You shouldn't date
with the assumption it will last."
And there I stood,
a fool, unmasked in my earnestness,
holding the fragile bird of commitment,
hoping it might grow wings.
But how easy it is
to dole out wisdom
from the safety of an anchored ship,
when your heart rests
on the promise of forever,
the certainty of a ring.
I wanted to say,
"Would you have said this
before your love was secure?
When your story was still a question,
not an answer?"
But my tongue held its breath,
too kind to cut her.
Why is it
that the one who dares

to love with their whole being
must endure the hardest lessons?
Why must the pure-hearted
face the bitter truth
while the guarded find their reward?
Still, I know this:
I'd rather love recklessly,
with the faith of a believer,
than live half-hearted,
hoarding my affections
like secrets meant to protect me.
For even if love faltered,
even if my heart bled for the loss,
I loved as if it could last,
and that is no foolish thing.

One Day

They tell me with a knowing grin,
"You'll find your man one day."
As if my life won't quite begin
Until he's on his way.
Their words drip with a sweet concern,
A pity laced with hope.
They think there's so much left to learn,
That I'm not whole alone.
But in the silence of my nights,
I dance beneath the stars.
I navigate my own delights,
Unhindered by their bars.
Perhaps one day love will arrive,
And perhaps it won't too.
But either way, I am alive,
My sky is wide and blue.
So spare me well-meant platitudes,
I'm writing my own song.
In solitude,
I've found my truths— I've been complete all along.

The Walls Around His Heart

He came to me, a traveler with no map,
A fortress of silence in his steadfast grasp.
His smile, a façade, his touch, a ghost,
A lover, yet a stranger I cherished most.
His walls stood high, impenetrable stone,
Guarding wounds he'd never shown.
I reached with tender hands, pleading to feel,
But his heart stayed locked, its gates of steel.
Our bodies met in rhythm, in need,
A hunger sated, but no heart freed.
Yes, it felt good—how could it not?
But passion, tenderness—it was all forgot.
The warmth of love was a distant flame,
Replaced by motions that bore no name.
Each kiss a script, each sigh rehearsed,
Leaving my soul aching, utterly immersed.
I longed for him, not just his skin,
To break the walls and let me in.
But he held his fortress firm and tight,
Shrouding his heart in eternal night.
Now I sit with the echo, a hollow ache,
The pieces of hope he didn't take.
And my heart weeps in its quiet despair,
For the love I offered, met with air.

Would he ever let me see the core?
Or must I ache for what's no more?
I loved him still, though he stood apart,
And mourned the walls around his heart.

Expiration Date

"Are you sure you're okay with just being friends?"
Your voice, soft, searching, it bends,
And I nod, a practiced smile on my face,
While inside, my heart frays, breaking at its base.
We had dared to dream beyond the screen,
Spilled our secrets in the in-between,
Life, love, fears, and fragile goals,
You held my words as if they were gold.
But when we met, it was touch, not trust,
Flesh, not forever—our desires combust.
Friends with benefits, a fragile disguise,
An expiration date loomed in your eyes.
Each kiss tasted like a fleeting flame,
Each touch whispered, "This won't remain."
And when the week folded into its close,
I lost not just you, but the part of me that knows.
Now silence hangs where laughter had thrived,
Our bond severed, our connection deprived.
How do I return to the life I had known,
When your ghost lingers in every room I own?
I replay your question, haunting my mind,
"Are you sure?"—but I lied, left the truth behind.
No, I was never okay, not even a bit,
Loving you in fragments, my heart won't admit.

The Airhead

I know I'm an airhead, it's painfully clear,
When the kitchen's a war zone I refuse to go near.
Recipes taunt me; the stove's like a test,
So I just make smoothies and hope for the best.
My mind runs in circles, anxious and loud,
Fearing the whispers of a judging crowd.
I'll replay conversations a thousand times,
Inventing critiques that exist in my mind.
And oh, my apartment—a cluttered domain,
A graveyard of clothes I'll never wear again.
I tell myself, "Sort them! Donate or sell!"
But instead, I just add to the fabric-filled hell.
Yet for all of my chaos, my stumbles, my quirks,
There's a soul that loves deeply and a heart that still
works.
I'll fumble, I'll fall, I'll forget, and I'll stress,
But I'll always give more when I've got less.
So judge me or love me, it's all just the same,
I'll own every flaw without any shame.
For being an airhead means living unplanned,
With a heart wide open and a helping hand.

The Kind Of Love That's Meant For Me

It began like waves crashing on a distant shore,
A wild, restless beauty I couldn't ignore.
He carried the salt air, the sun in his hair,
But the tide revealed truths I wasn't prepared to bear.
In his laughter, I found fleeting delight,
But shadows emerged in the quiet of night.
Promises whispered, like foam on the sand,
Vanished as quickly as they met my hand.
Yet, from this ebb, I learned to see,
The kind of love that's meant for me.
A partner who mirrors the rhythm I crave,
Who dances with tides, both fearless and brave.
A surfer boy, the ocean in his veins,
With a passion for life that never wanes.
Fit and strong, with a steady stride,
Who inspires me to walk by his side.
Not just a lover, but my truest friend,
With dreams that align, like paths that blend.
He'll share my longing for adventure untamed,
A pirate at heart, unafraid and unchained.
He'll call me his queen, his compass, his guide,
And treat me with passion that never subsides.
With patience and kindness, he'll weather the storms,

Holding me close when the seas transform.
His love will be fierce, yet tender and true,
Unconditional in all that we do.
He'll see my fire, my dreams, my art,
And cherish the wildness that lives in my heart.
Together we'll roam with sails unfurled,
Claiming our treasures in a boundless world.
Through sunsets ablaze and skies painted blue,
He'll love me as deeply as the ocean's hue.
From disappointment grew clarity,
A deeper understanding of what's meant for me.
The Sea has its lessons, the waves their role,
In shaping my vision, in guiding my soul.
For I know the man I'll one day see—
He'll crown me his Pirate Queen and sail life's seas with
me.